Among the Believers

For Michael,

Thanks so much for allowing me to be part of this exciting program. All best in art and life.

Ron 5/30/01

Among the Believers

Ron Rash

IRIS PRESS
Oak Ridge, Tennessee
www.irisbooks.com

cover photograph: Jo Stafford

book design: Robert B. Cumming, Jr.

Acknowledgements

These poems have appeared in the following journals:

American Literary Review: "The Ascent"
Black Buzzard Review: "Woodshed"
Blueline: "October on Middlefork Creek"
Carolina Quarterly: "Madison County, 1864"
Chattahoochee Review: "Air and Angels"
Cumberland Poetry Review: "Barn Loft: 1959," "On
   the Border"
*45/96: The Ninety-Six Sampler of South Carolina
   Poetry*: "Winter Lightning"
Georgia Review: "Flood"
Mars Hill Literary Review: "Blue River"
Mossy Creek Reader: "Last Rite," "Appalachian
   Christ," "Interment," "Foot Washing." "In a
   Springhouse at Night," "Decoration Day," "North
   of Asheville"
New England Review: "The Fox"
Now and Then: "The Preacher Is Called To Testify for
   the Accused," "Watershed"
Pembroke Magazine: "Return," "The Bridge"
Prairie Schooner: "Ginseng," "Lasting Water"
South Carolina Review: "The Barn," "Catamount,"
   "Graveyard Fields"
Southern Poetry Review: "In Middlefork Gorge"
Southern Review: "Among the Believers," "A Preacher
   Who Takes Up Serpents Laments the Presence of
   Skeptics at His Church," "Good Friday, 1995,
   Driving Westward," "Harvest," "Sunday Evening
   at Middlefork Pentecostal Church," "Animal
   Hides"

Texas Review: "Abandoned Homestead in Watauga County"

Virginia Quarterly Review: "Morning Service: August 1959," "The Exchange"

Weber State Studies: "The Skeleton in the Dogwood," "The Well"

The author thanks the following for their support and advice while writing these poems: Cathy Smith Bowers, Terry Hall, Jeff Daniel and Linda Parsons Marion, Robert Morgan, Ann Rash, Mark Swanson, Frederick Shilstone, faculty, staff, and administration at Tri-County Technical College, and the National Endowment for the Arts.

In Memory of my father
James Hubert Rash — believer

Let me forget nothing now,
In this hour of losing...

— George Scarbrough
from "Summer Revival"

A Gift Matched
with Skills of the First Order

This extraordinary volume of poems must be savored and relished one poem at a time, the way we always address any book of poems, most usually finding treasures and delights that especially please us, like plums in a pudding. But this collection I find utterly and astonishingly different. The poems individually are of the highest quality, without doubt; and to find a book composed so uniformly and unfalteringly of excellent poems is, by itself, a stunning experience. But what seems to me the supreme achievement in Mr. Rash's work inheres in a quality derived partly from his remarkable skill, partly from the richness of his regional past, largely from his dramatic instincts, stoic voice, and deep humanity, that have created here not so much a collection of poems as something with the coherence of a perfectly composed novella — a long account by, say, Chekhov or Faulkner, Eudora Welty or Flannery O'Connor. It has no plot, to be sure. There is no sustained story, suspense, intricacy of interwoven actions. But there is emphatically a pervading and presiding atmosphere: what, in a Hardy novel, would be embodied in a landscape expressive of the destiny of all his characters or dramatis personae, a symbolism that infuses all the lives he creates.

Of Mr. Rash's technical skills careful notice needs to be taken. He is a master of his own kind of syllabic verse, quite different from the way other poets in recent times have employed it. He opens this collection with a number of poems written in seven-syllable lines, a pattern he favors throughout. Here is one, for example, that exhibits his special kind of excellence.

The Corpse Bird

Bed-sick she heard the bird's call
fall soft as a pall that night
quilts tightened around her throat,
her grey eyes narrowed, their light
gone as she saw what she'd heard
waiting for her in the tree
cut down at daybreak by kin
to make the coffin, bury
that perch around her so death
might find one less place to rest.

What moves and impresses in these lines is related to a dramatic use of enjambment, to the poet's ability to force us beyond a point at which we had expected to rest in accepted resolution, and deliberately to confound a cluster of events: the fact of her "seeing" what she has heard as the light departs from her eyes (emphasized by the ambiguity of "narrowed," which can be read as either a verb or an adjective); that what she sees is in the tree that at dawn will be cut down to make a coffin, not alone to serve for burial but to remove a perch where death might rest at some future time; the wonderful ambiguity of time on "that night/quilts tightened around her throat..." Was this simultaneous with the narrowing of her eyes? with her seeing what she'd heard? At what point in this elaborate series of events does she actually die? The lines, the small events, blend and flow together in a seamless utterance that is full of mystery and drama. The poem abounds in internal rhymes: call, fall, pall; night, tightened; kin, coffin. Moreover, a poet who can begin a poem called "The Preacher is Called to Testify for the Accused" with the following lines,

Before the just Lord raised this world's foundations,
centered the sun, speckled the heavens with stars,
before He dredged the land out of the water,
molded Adam's limbs from dust and spit,
God knew the time would come when Isaac Hampton
would drink too much one night but not before
he won in a poker game no bills or coins,
no ring or saddle but an owlshead pistol
he didn't want or need.

knows what he's doing in something approaching the grand manner, albeit in an American, rural version. There is an exuberance, a sheer gusto to these lines that brings to mind Mark Twain and some of the improvisatory spell-binders among his fictional characters.

It may be that a reader will find suspect my continued references to works and authors of fiction in characterizing some of the qualities of Mr. Rash's poetry; and I would have to admit that the names I've dropped around him are all of my own choosing, and they may have had no actual role in the shaping of his special sensibility. But I can at least point to the fact that in 1987 he won a Younger Writers Award for fiction; and perhaps it may be useful as well as timely now to say something about his background.

His family has lived in the southern Appalachian mountains since the mid-1700's, and a knowledge and feel for this region, its folklore, faiths, superstitions, loyalties and culture, is an abiding presence in his poems. He was born in Chester, South Carolina in 1953, grew up in Boiling Springs, North Carolina, and now lives with a wife and two children in Clemson, South Carolina, where he supports himself and his family by teaching. He has a bachelor's and a master's degree in English, and has published one previous volume of poems, *Eureka Mill*, and has another completed, even before this goes to press. Such remarkable fertility is the more impressive in that it has been sustained under the burden of a teaching load of five or six classes, mostly in freshman composition.

In the face of all this, perhaps in defiance of it, he has managed to write one of the most dazzlingly exalted and ecstatic love poems I know, called "Ploughing on Moonlight." And there is another joyful poem about, I assume, some earlier Rash in his family, a poem called "The Exchange." But it must be acknowledged that the general tenor of these poems is somber and sometimes stark, though occasionally lit with a wonderful comic irony. Mr. Rash's poetic sources (as distinct from his conjectured fictional ones) are highly sophisticated and somewhat exotic. His family background is Welsh, and he knows as much as Robert Graves about Welsh poetics and *The Mabinogion,* and has aimed at times at that kind of alliteration the Welsh call *cynghanedd.* It seems to me that I detect something Scottish in his work as well. But certainly Hopkins and possibly Frost lie behind some of his finest achievements. And any poet audacious enough to title one of his poems "Air and Angels" is pointing with a justified pride to a distinguished ancestry.

I have found myself so deeply impressed by the richness and variety of Mr. Rash's poems in *Among the Believers* that I must deliberately restrain myself from continuing to quote with happy abandon those poems I especially like (there are too many), but I can't close without singling out one of them, an absolutely amazing monologue, full of terror, showmanship, bizarre and possibly insane faith, and yet for all that a credible and absolute predestinate conviction. The eeriness of this poem, "A Preacher Who Takes Up Serpents Laments the Presence of Skeptics in His Church," lies in its triumphantly appropriated voice. It begins:

> Every sabbath they come,
> gawk like I'm something
> in a tent at a county fair.
> In the vanity of their unbelief
> they will cover an eye with a camera
> and believe it will make them see.
> They see nothing. I show them Mark: 16
> but they believe in the word of man.
> They believe death is an end.

But fine as this poem is, it can by no means represent the versatility, amplitude, and general tenor of Mr. Rash's work. His is a talent that can deal in his poems with high drama, filled at times with violence, but at others with a quiet, unsettling mystery. He employs a rich density of language and dignity of utterance, though sometimes his dramatic monologues adopt a suitable vernacular. Yet they all abound with clarity of observation and accuracy of feeling, employing powerful and marvelously apt metaphors. My admiration for this achievement is without limit, and in my view this book deserves the enthusiastic notice of anyone interested in American poetry.

— Anthony Hecht

CONTENTS

I

ON THE BORDER

Today it's still hard country,
bare hills, dark valleys, gray juts
of stone against gray sky. Here
men argued map lines with blood,

raised death like a seed crop when
their hearts became their landscape,
as did their acts. One winter
after days of murders, rapes,

burned homesteads, ransacked churches,
a band of reivers turned back
north to the last wide water
before the border, their backs

laden with golden crosses,
chalices that dragged them down
halfway across and they drowned
in a river called Eden.

THE SKELETON IN THE DOGWOOD
(Watauga County, 1895)

Two lovers out walking found
more than spring's promised blessing
on new beginnings hanging
in a dogwood tree's branches.

No friend or kin claimed those bones.
The high sheriff came. Foul play
he was sure, but how or why
he found no answers, so stayed

to help break the ground, help haul
a flat rock out of the creek,
sprinkle some dirt, some God words,
then left for more recent crimes.

The lovers wed that winter.
On their marriage night they dreamed
of bouquets of spring flowers
blooming in a dead man's hand.

SCARECROW

He said this land would kill him,
and when it did his widow
left the hoe where he dropped it
on his death-row, staked his clothes

to raise his stark shade over
tall corn stalks like the black pall
she laid across his casket.
All that summer, into fall

she allowed no harrowing plow
where his heart failed, not until
five Aprils passed and the last
rag on that rotting cross fell.

PLOWING ON MOONLIGHT

I rose with the moon, left the drowsy sheets,
my nine months wife singing in her sleep,
left boots on the floor, overalls and hat
scarecrowing a bedpost so I could plant
my seeds with just a plow between
the earth and me, my pale feet sunk deep
in the ridged wake where I labored,
gripped the handles like a divining rod,
my eyes closed to the few stars out
glittering like mica in a creek. All night
I plowed, limbs pebbled, beard budded by frost,
my chest nippled, my breath blooming white,
and knew again the sway of the sea,
the flow of river, the smallest creek,
rain's pelt and soak, the taproot's thrust,
the cicada's winged resurrection.
I opened my eyes to dawnlight,
left my field and lay with my wife,
warming as I pressed against her body,
my hand listening to her waxing belly.

FLOOD

No river on the sixth day, just a sprawl
of water laking across the bottomland.
Barns wandered from farms like overturned arks.
Fences drowned, boundaries disappeared.
I found a canoe, paddled out to the oak
that anchored my far pasture, the only place
high enough for a miracle, a bull or cow
knee-deep and bawling, hungry but alive.
I could not find the world I knew. It seemed
time had coiled back to the old beginning:
garfish thrashed the surface, loggerheads
sank into their helmets as I circled
the pasture and found no cattle, just the oak,
its face rising into a sky so low
the rattlesnakes that swayed among the branches
were only limbs away from gaining heaven.

Winter Lightning

When lightning struck the big oak, cracked
and splintered Curt's deer stand, he ignored
the older hunters back at camp
who spoke of winter lightning as if more
than natural and swore it best
seen as a sign more ominous
than an owl at noon. The oak was now cursed,
bad enough to touch it, much less
spend time perched high in its limbs.
Curt rebuilt his stand the next morning,
and stayed up there despite the warning,
until he fell and broke his neck.
The man who found him closed his eyes,
then left to notify his kin.
An accident, some said, although
none climbed the tree to fetch his gun.

THE CONFESSION

She hacked the throat of her child
with a knife more rust than steel,
later told how her arm tired
as the windpipe slipped the blade
so dug instead for the heart,
then noosed a rock to the corpse,
threw it into a blue hole,
where it stayed until set free
by high water to be left
shored on a sandbar downstream
until the high sheriff brought
his suspect for some believed
a sign might make known her guilt
in the last gaze but the eyes
were shut though the mouth was not,
filling that cold mouth a bloom
of yellowjackets that flew
straight from the lips of her child
to hers like a whispered kiss
burning until the truth hived
in her heart rose to her lips,
and though upon the scaffold
she spoke an hour what most
remembered was the word stung
from her tongue on a sandbar,
and that one word was murder.

THE CORPSE BIRD

Bed-sick she heard the bird's call
fall soft as a pall that night
quilts tightened around her throat,
her gray eyes narrowed, their light
gone as she saw what she'd heard
waiting for her in the tree
cut down at daybreak by kin
to make the coffin, bury
that perch around her so death
might find one less place of rest.

Madison County: 1864

No civil war could be fought
where bloodlines and creeks named sides,
ancestral grudges freed
an intimate politics
of atrocity, so men
authored new testaments from
Jehovah's old laws when they
raised enemies toward heaven
like offerings to be found years
later in hollows and glens,
dangling bones like drawn buckets
above a well, if cut down
left on the ground where they fell,
food for wild hogs. Once a hand
came waving out of the woods
held in a hound's yellow growl,
and down in Shelton Laurel
Widow Franklin told her sons
If you die, die like a dog,
your teeth in somebody's throat.

ALLEN'S COMMAND

After his hands buried son
and daughter, Colonel Allen
gathered men and boys he blamed,
let them huddle like cattle
two days and nights as snow fell,
wind bared the beneath of rags,
then marched them up Knoxville Road
to a meadow where no prayer
was asked or answered, where red
blossomed the snow like something
come too soon. Those fortunate
died from musket balls, the rest
hoe-hacked like snakes, their one grave
danced on to push them deeper
into hell, and for decades
mothers in Shelton Laurel
knew mention of Allen's name
would quiet the surliest son.

ON THE WATAUGA

On the bank of a river
he saw a tall tree, one half
crimson fire from root to crown,
the other half green with leaves.
All night the firelight colored
the river red as a wound.
A full moon loomed as he walked
into the waist-deep water,
bathed and tugged by a current
flickering like a cold flame
until the stars dimmed like sparks,
the tall tree's heat lit the sun,
and he staggered to the shore
white-eyed, blinded by Godlight.

BEFORE

Before clock hands showed the time
time ceased, and looking-glasses
were veiled as if they still held
familiar faces, in those
last moments when breath shallowed
like a wellspring running dry,
God-words quickened, only then
the dying left death-beds borne
on the arms of the gathered,
lowered to the floor so they
might press close, as though a door
through which to listen and know
the earth's old secrets before
it opened, and they entered.

THE EXCHANGE

Between Wytheville, Virginia
and the North Carolina line,
he meets a wagon headed
where he's been, seated beside
her parents a dark-eyed girl
who grips the reins in her fist,
no more than sixteen, he'd guess
as they come closer and she
doesn't look away or blush
but allows his eyes to hold
hers that moment their lives pass.
He rides into Boone at dusk,
stops at an inn where he buys
his supper, a sleepless night
thinking of fallow fields still
miles away, the girl he might
not find the like of again.
When dawn breaks he mounts his roan,
then backtracks, searches three days
hamlets and farms, any smoke
rising above the tree line
before he heads south, toward home,
the French Broad's valley where spring
unclinches the dogwood buds
as he plants the bottomland,
come night by candlelight builds
a butter churn and cradle,
cherry headboard for the bed,
forges a double-eagle
into a wedding ring and then
back to Virginia and spends
five weeks riding and asking

from Elk Creek to Damascas
before he finds the wagon
tethered to the hitching post
of a crossroads store, inside
the girl who smiles as if she'd
known all along his gray eyes
would search until they found her.
She asks one question, his name,
as her eyes study the gold
smoldering there between them,
the offered palm she lightens,
slips the ring on herself so
he knows right then the woman
she will be, bold enough match
for a man rash as his name.

II

A Preacher Who Takes Up Serpents
Laments the Presence of Skeptics in His
Church

Every sabbath they come,
gawk like I'm something
in a tent at a county fair.
In the vanity of their unbelief
they will cover an eye with a camera
and believe it will make them see.
They see nothing. I show them Mark: 16
but they believe in the word of man.
They believe death is an end.

And would live like manure maggots,
wallow in the filth of man's creation.
Less than a mile from here
the stench of sulpher rises
like fog off the Pigeon River.
They do not believe it is a sign
of their own wickedness.
They cannot see a river
is a vein in God's arm.

When I open the wire cages
they back away like crayfish
and tell each other I am insane —
terrified I may not be.

Others, my own people, whisper
"He tempts God," and will not join me.
They cannot understand surrender
is humility, not arrogance,
that a man afraid to die cannot live.

Only the serpents sense the truth.
The diamondback's blunted tail is silent,
the moccasin's pearl-white mouth closed.
The coral snake coils around
my wrist, a harmless bright bracelet,
in the presence of the Lord.

Decoration Day

One whose hand could make a face
out of paper and pencil
would lay the glassed black and whites
on the communion table,
trace our dead kin back to life
to walk this land they once walked
and see again, through our eyes,
the dogwoods, ash trees, and oaks,
swift flowing creeks, narrow skies,
peaks and coves in memory mapped
so deep not even heaven
could wish them from looking back.

SUNDAY EVENING AT MIDDLEFORK CREEK
PENTECOSTAL CHURCH

Like poets, they know a fallen world's
words fail a pure vision,
so would wrench from the heart
a new language, and feel
sound pour from their mouths
like a hemorrhage, and fall
white-eyed to the concrete floor,
epileptic in the ecstasy
of the word made flesh.

FOOT WASHING

He who once walked water knelt
to first cleanse feet, then souls of men,
so we have gathered once again
on the bank where spring's warm light
falls like grace through willow leaves,
golds the river where we bend,
to fill our washpans so we might
follow in His footsteps on our knees.

THE LANGUAGE OF CANAAN

If dawn caught and dazzled on
dew beads strung to spider's web,
sweep of shadow crossed meadow
like calming hand, it might come —
luxuriant bloom of assurance
grafted onto tongue, language
graced with a cadence so pure
ears deaf a lifetime now heard,
and for decades afterward
whole settlements would visit
streamside, meadow, that place one
world bled into another.

The Afflicted

My elders would speak of those who could not,
whose vocabulary of verb and noun
never took root, grew sentences,
as afflicted, yet also blessed in
one way always significant.
Skill with saw, guitar or horse,
a strong back, pleasing face or just
a kind disposition would be enough.
Families back then would wait for years
for that one talent to come to light,
confirming the attentive eye,
the marked child marked in God's favor.

The Preacher is Called to Testify
for the Accused

Before a just Lord raised this world's foundations,
centered the sun, speckled the heavens with stars,
before He dredged the land out of the water,
molded Adam's limbs from dust and spit,
God knew the time would come when Isaac Hampton
would drink too much one night but not before
he won in a poker game no bills or coins,
no ring or saddle but an owlshead pistol
he didn't want or need. Collateral
was all it was, was all it *seemed* to be.
And though he'd won no money he'd lost none,
though down to his last dime when Jacob Lunsford
dealt him two straight aces and Isaac won
his drinking money back, the owlshead pistol.
Those cards were stacked but not by Jacob Lunsford.
So Isaac Hampton bought the moonshine whiskey
he thought to carry home but ended up
drinking with his best friend Ezra Whitfield
on the riverbank in late November
because no cold wind sent them home, no rain
fell from heaven until the morning came.
These are facts. They cannot be disputed.
We've all heard the sheriff's testimony.
The night was "strangely warm," his words, not mine.
And why was Ezra on that riverbank,
a man not much for drink except this night?
His brahma bull had died that afternoon.
As surely as He led us to this courtroom,
God had led that bull up to the springhouse
to gorge itself on laurel that would kill it
not three days before or three days after

November nineteenth, 1923.
That's why Ezra walked out of that hollow
on Sunday night when any other Sunday
he'd be in church, not off to town to try
and drink away the pain, the memory
of two months sweat left in his neighbor's field
to buy a bull he'd only owned a week.
And though there were two paths he could have taken
he took the one that followed Middlefork
although the other path was better worn,
had fewer roots to trip on in the dark.
God brought Ezra Whitfield down that trail,
brought Isaac up from town, the moonshine whiskey
waiting to be drunk, the owlshead pistol
crouching like a panther in his pocket.
Isaac almost home. In five more minutes
he'd have left the river trail and followed
the creek up Dismal Mountain. That did not happen.
For they had crossed God's path. We know the rest,
or think we know, the drunken argument
the grievous wound, the water in the lungs.
We know no more than water spiders know
the depths of pools they skate across. Like them
we live upon the surface. Things occur
we have no inkling of. All we can know
is God's watch measured Ezra Whitfield's time
so Isaac Hampton's crime was our Lord's will,
which is no crime unless our pride would judge
the apple's fall, the barn owl's dark, clawed sight,
the weasel's fierce appetite, this son
I fathered so our Father's will might raise
a rusty owlshead pistol to the chest
of Ezra Whitfield, Isaac's closest friend.
Judge me as well. I have my role in this.

Had I not lain with his mother years ago,
we'd not be here now. Men called it sin
to lie with her but it was God's design
that we should bring this child into the world,
so judge as well the ones who begot me,
take it back a hundred generations,
all the way to He who begot Adam.
For there is where it ends, where it begins.
We must believe in providence and see
good where only evil seems to be.
If Judas had not kissed our savior's cheek
Christ would not have died on Calvary,
redeemed us with his blood. No earthly man
did a greater good. It's my belief
that Judas walks the golden paths of heaven.
These words I speak, they too are preordained
to sway or not to sway. If my son hangs
he dies like Judas died but unlike Judas
not by his own hand, condemned like Christ
by men who thought their actions justified.

GRAVEYARD FIELDS

Four hundred cattle died the winter
six feet of snow renamed this meadow.
They did not die in silence. Hunger
echoed through the hollows where men
huddled in front of hearths, listened
five days, four nights before they gathered
at Shining Rock Creek, then staggered
through glare and drifts into the valley,
but not before emptying cribs, lofts,
burdening their backs, the backs of mules.
They found what they already knew,
calmed the mules, scattered the vultures,
spread out among the carcasses
salt licks and corn, the ricks of hay,
offered knowing their Testament claimed
such creatures soulless, unsaved.

III

SIGNS

My older kin always believed
in looking backward to explain
the here and now, always a sign
present in the past each time

a barn burned down, a life was lost.
So like boys turning over stones
to find what dark had hid from day,
they'd turn over in their minds

the way a mare turned from its stall
as if she smelled hay smoldering,
a living hand so damp and cold
it seemed already in the grave.

And so I learned to see the world
as language one might understand
but only when translated by
signs first forgotten or misread.

ANIMAL HIDES

As if in flight they ascend
on barn-back, shed-side: bobcat
and fox, raccoon and black bear,
limbs splayed as if gliding on
wind-lift as coats dry and tan
to become somehow more than
brag of well-hid trap, true aim,
a poor man's taxidermy —
for they remain when weathered
into fur-scrap, pelt-shadow
ghosting across graying boards,
as though their death-hurriers
kenned animal once meant soul,
like those first hunters believe
some essence may yet linger,
must be earth-freed, given wing.

THE ASCENT

Some thought she had slipped, the plank
glazed slick with ice, or maybe
already cold beyond care,
drowsy and weary, bare feet
tempting a creekbed's promise
of sleep, though she struggled out,
her trail a handprint of stars
rising toward a dazzle of white
where sun and snow met. They found
her homespun dress, underclothes,
before they found her, her eyes
open as the sky, as cold,
as far away. Her father
climbed the nearest tree, brought down
green sprigs, berries bright as blood,
weaved a garland for her brow,
and that was how they left her,
wearing a crown, unburied,
knowing they'd never hunt here
or build a cabin where she
undressed, left their world as death
closed around her like a room
and she lay down on the snow,
a bride awaiting her groom.

NORTH OF ASHEVILLE

Dark flooded the lake before
the grabbling hook tore flesh snagged
on tree-fall, flashlights cast light
like life-ropes as if what dragged
in the searcher's wake could yet
be brought back, for that was what
they believed, those on the shore
since morning, who'd gathered that
spring dawn so the sun might rise
above lives saved by water,
and was why the child's mother
refused the undertaker
three days and nights as they prayed
and sang praise, lifted Bibles
toward heaven, waved God's promise
as if to guide down angels.
Because they could not wake him,
the fourth day she surrendered
his body to the earth, though
she swore come night what woke her
was no dream, that he had returned
to his birth-bed, his shirt sleeves
dripping as he lay warm hands
on hers so she might believe.

Last Rite

No one could say exactly where he died,
(just why and how: his murderer confessed)
no stream or peak to mark a county line,
homesteaders near enough who might be asked,
if eastern Tennessee or Carolina,
although they knew the place, his skillet nailed
into a tree a few steps off the trail.
Three years passed. A surveyor was sought out,
a Buncombe County man who led his mare
into the valley south of Laurel Cove,
followed the dead man's brothers, his widow who
    shared
a mount with her first-born son and second husband,
the mother last, a Bible in her hand.
The surveyor stumbled up the nearest ridge.
An hour later he came back and wrote
four words to end two journeys, just below
the date and place of birth, the date of death:
Watauga County, North Carolina.

Harvest

Our shovels and mattocks clattered and clanged
as the truck hugged the mountain, lunged and curved
away from the church, a morning spent
to break and heave that rocky ground,
burying ourselves to bury him.

That afternoon we came again,
listened to the preacher's words,
while a hurrying sky spilled leaves across
the high-stoned, sudden-flowered earth,
reminding us of things undone.

We changed and roughly smoothed the grave
so we might kneel in fall's last light
out in his field, our butcher knives
raising heads of cabbage from the ground.

IN THE SOLOMONS

A bone-deep kind of knowing
old hunters claimed — those moments
before antlers bloomed alive
in thicket, rose from ground fog
like something long buried — how
they sensed a presence as though
conjured and so sure would thumb
safeties and aim, and when war
carried my uncle from blue
ridges of North Carolina
to green pacific atolls,
he felt his life-taker perched
above in a blur of leaf,
and when nothing fell had climbed
to confirm, found the sniper
roped to the tree, gun branch-hung,
and one thing more, not a gold
buddha but a gold cross worn
over the dead man's heart on
that God-forsaken fist-thrust
of coral where from that moment
my uncle trusted only
his soul to Christ, trusted life
to an older believing.

RETURN

Gaunt and silent, pale,
my uncle seems the ghost
a lower aim would have made
as he steps off the train
into the truck, inside
his father and sister who
slid and braked ten miles
down the mountain to Boone,
snow falling as it has
since noon. The road disappears
before they're halfway home.
My uncle walks point, shoulders
his duffel bag, shadows
Middlefork to the pool
where Holder Branch enters,
follows the creek up the mountain,
through the step-muffling snow,
past church and graveyard. Soon
the last light starts to fade.
The snow blurs blue. He sees
the candle in the window,
unknots the bag, removes
the bullet-nicked helmet, walks
across the pasture to the spring,
breaks the ice and drinks.

FROM *The Mabinogion*

Having twice traveled the sea,
battle-bloodied, swords bone-dulled,
Branwen buried inside her
square-sided grave, having heard
the three birds of Rhiannon,
they came into a great hall —
sea-facing, hero worthy,
two doors wide open, one closed,
and like snow warmed by the sun
all they had seen and suffered
melted away. No sorrow
could harbor inside that hall.
No beard grayed, night and day merged
into vast fields of twilight
beyond time, though a time came
they chose to open the door.
A cold sea stung their faces.
Memory settled like ravens
upon their shoulders: kinsmen
and friends who died by their side,
woes of age, old wounds, heart grief
whose sudden weight so staggered
they wondered it ever borne,
and knew they were finally home.

IV

In a Springhouse at Night

Candle-dim flickering shadows, orange
salamanders flare across floorstone,
water troughed, held like gutterswell.
Cabbage and beets, beans and sweet corn
fill the walls. Grandmother's tall
hands lighten shelves. My fingers braille
springflow verbing: unearthed, sprung.

BLUE RIVER

One Saturday afternoon
my father raised a paint brush,
to make the River Jordan
run through the Carolina hills.
I lay on a pew, followed
the whispered hymns the brush made
as it swept across the wall,
and that blue river rose high
as purple windows darkened
into bruises, root-shadows
seeped from the corners, deepened
the baptistry. It was like
my father drowned as his arm
reached up, finished the far shore,
as if his hand a last wave
before he sank in the pool
where grown men fell and gasped while
hallelujahs shook the church,
the place where I would fall too
on some soon-coming Sunday,
washed away in a current
raised by my father's right hand.

SPRING LIZARDS

We could not keep them in jars
with star-pricked lids or fishhook
their lips, cast them into the
deep pools of Middlefork Creek,
though we might gently scoop up
the rough-skinned newts, mud puppies,
sleek salamanders, ours for
a few seconds, then set free,
sipped under rusty tin that
roofed the spring's source, the hidden
earth-water we'd always heard
their presence had blessed, made pure.

The Well

Tangled, snaky, a homestead
to stay far from, and a well
where some claimed if you listened
you'd hear howling up from hell
the scorched voice of Carl Gragstone,
who dug that well, broke that land
then a wife who hanged herself
from the barn's highest beam, and
this was the place that I came
one May afternoon alone,
waded through thorn-snatch, sumac
to hear for myself and leaned
my ear to dark, brushed the noose
that swung the rust-rotten pail,
listened and listened and heard
not a single sound until
I cupped my mouth with my hands
and called, "Hello, Carl Gragstone,
are you down in hell?" and heard
not his damned words but my own.

AIR AND ANGELS

I loved the way the sun struck
like a match and they surfaced
from purple gloam as though they
might pass right through those windows:
the wide-winged seraphims, robed
and haloed, their hair a flow
of gold, thin images pressed
against glass like butterflies.
But they stayed outside our world,
although air stirred like wing beats
each time my sweaty hand raised
a Jones Funeral Home fan
and an angel's face leaned close
enough to whisper my name.

WATERSHED

I could not see, even say
what it was my aunt explained
with a word, a nod beyond
the slant of pasture, the end
of family land. I supposed
a weave of wood and tin used
by thirsty hunters, maybe
the lost, or a child like me
willing to straddle barbed wire,
go where just sky rose higher,
to find nothing built, instead
a barn-tall rock whose face shed
wrinkles of water like tears
I rubbed between my fingers
like the blind girl whose first word
flowed out from the underworld
through well-pump onto her hand
before it could be sounded.

GINSENG

Even midday the mountain's
north face was veiled in shadows,
a place to stay lost, as once
an old woman had, her ghost
still trying to get back home,
where others lived. It was here
my grandfather searched each fall
the deep coves, the gloam under
cliffhangs where yellow leaves pooled
so bright it seemed what sun had
scattered in since spring was held
until October, then freed
to light the virid stem-wings
into a brief golden star.
I went with him once, our words
kept low, almost a whisper
as we shook free the pale roots
from black loam, planted the seeds
and going back home had crossed
where two boulders squeezed the creek
to a slick white rush, crossed there
where no ghost dared to follow.

LASTING WATER

After fingers raked out the caul
of black leaves, and spring lizards
scuttled and settled like things
blown by the wind, only then
would my grandfather savor
that spurt water makes in sand
as it breaks free from the world's
underneath to pool and spread
across the land like skyroots
even in the direst drought.
He called it *lasting water*,
that low-pulsed flow he scooped up
with blistered palms so it might
touch his lips as he kneeled there
at the field's edge where corn rows
withered like paper in flames,
limp rags of tobacco burned
without a match and green wings
sang in the trees to bring rain.

PASSAGE

Even raised from their lost world,
captured in Life's late-fifties
suburban gloss, those cave prints
kept their power — animals
flowing like strange dreams across
veldts of limestone, human hand
hovering on the wall like flame,
something intranslatable
no camera could bring to light,
so that spring I searched the cave
above Goshen Creek, my lamp
wood-wick burning to thumb
before dropped, another struck,
waved over walls like a brush,
but no sabertooth, bison
muscled that dark, nothing there
but a hunter's old campfire,
so I let my last match die,
imagined walls come alive,
hoof and paw circling, one hand
raised among them in welcome.

THE BARN

Outside on the graying wood
the hides of fox and raccoon
stretch and yawn in death.
We enter the barn's cool darkness,
wait for sight to return, listening
to the mud dauber's tuneless song,
the blacksnake sliding across loose straw.

My grandfather coughs into his handkerchief
a dark-red mass like a piece of his heart.
He will be dead in a month. Each day
his gaunt face grows gaunter.
Doctor, wife, children — they want him in bed,
so he has brought me,
to check his sons' work, to confirm
enough hay has been bailed for the winter.

He climbs the creaking ladder to the loft,
resting every other rung.
I am too young to follow, can only hear
the scrape of his brogan workboots
as he moves above, counting, calculating.
Satisfied, he leads me out
into the world of light.

WOODSHED

The door swung shut. Cold and dark
surrounded like deep water
as I waited for moat-glow
to settle like dust, bring back
the hams hung like hornet's nests,
winter's fire piled high as smoke,
thin shed of snakeskin, a fox
sprung free from a rusty trap
on the wall, and when it all,
or almost all, had returned,
I raised my grandfather's axe,
dreamed of that first spark of light
breaking into his coffin.

Barn Loft: 1959

So still I can hear the heat
sear the tin, the barn swallow
weave its nest out of slant-light.
From shadows that smell like straw,
I watch corn rows ripple far
as Parkson's Cove, the scarecrow
raise his arms, wade the green waves,
and that word the preacher spoke
comes clear through the July haze
as though the writing spider
has caught time, suspended there
between an E and a Y.

THE FOX

Two months before he died my uncle saw
a red fox at the edge of the field he plowed,
watching him, its tongue unpanting though
the August heat-haze waved the air like water.

That night he claimed it was his father, then laughed
as if he wasn't serious, as if
all summer long we hadn't watched his face
grow old too quick, gray-stubbled, sudden-lined.

His wife would try the last days that he lived
to get him to the hospital but he
took to his bed, awaited the approach
of padded feet, coming close, then closer.

IN MIDDLEFORK GORGE

The white smoke of my own breath
led me down the logging road,
the sky darkening like a bruise.
I was too proud to be cold,

my first time hunting alone,
passed-on rifle in my hand,
walking ground that once belonged
to my family, now game land,

the logging road winding down
into the gorge, hard weather
leaning in from Tennessee,
cold and deep as a glacier.

Flakes fell like ashes as I
passed my grandfather's homestead,
its cairn of broken chimney,
scrub oaks where a barn once stood,

the gorge leveling out and then
a sudden, frost-scythed meadow,
the marble slabs like bleached stumps.
A clock was raised on hearthstone,

set in cement to weather
time but now all time erased,
each numbered hour swept away,
the hands torn free from the face.

August, 1959: Morning Service

Beside the open window
on the cemetery side,
I drowsed as Preacher Lusk gripped
his Bible like a bat snagged
from the pentecostal gloom.
In that room where heat clabbered
like churned butter, my eyes closed,
freed my mind into the light
on the window's other side,
followed the dreamy bell-ring
of Randy Ford's cows across
Licklog Creek to a spring pool
where orange salamanders swirled
and scuttled like flames. It was
not muttered words that urged me
back to that church, nor was it
the hard comfort of pews rowed
like the gravestones of my kin,
but the a cappelia hymn
sung by my great-aunt, this years
before the Smithsonian
taped her voice as if the song
of some vanishing species,
which it was, which all songs are,
years before the stroke wrenched her
face into a gnarled silence,
this morning before all that
she led us across Jordan,
and the gravestones leaned as if
even the dead were listening.

V

Abandoned Homestead
in Watauga County

All that once was is this,
shattered glass, a rot
of tin and wood, the hum
of limp-legged wasps that ascend
like mote swirls in the heatlight.

Out front a cherry tree
buckles in fruit, harvested
by yellowjackets and starlings,
the wind, the rain, and the sun.

THE BRIDGE

Barbed wire snags like briars when
fence posts rot in goldenrod,
the cows are gone, the cowpath
a thinning along the creek
to follow upstream until
water narrows, gray planks lean
over the flow like a book
open but left unfinished,
like this bridge was when the man
who started it took to his
death-bed, watched from there a son
drive the last nails, drive the truck
across so he might die less
burdened that night. The farmhouse
is razed now, the barn and shed
bare quilts of ground. All that's left
some fallen-down four by fours,
a few rusty nails, this bridge
the quick or the dead can't cross.

INTERMENT

My cousin comes this morning
in denim, brogans, not yet
the suit ironed last night, dark shoes
taken out of the closet.
A mattock, then a shovel
deepens what he, other men
almost finished yesterday
before Hawk Ridge snuffed the sun
and they latched the gate and he
volunteered to work alone
this scawmy October dawn,
finish up. To know it's done
he levels his right hand out
like a salute and measures
himself against the hole, deep
enough so flings the mattock
and shovel back to the world,
open ground where soon a Cook-
Hampton Funeral Home tent
will huddle the stone-gap black.
A year out of Vietnam,
he will stand a moment here
where he might have lain, then raise
himself from his father's grave.

BENEATH KEOWEE

Dammed waters lapped eaves like fire.
Soon just the spire could be seen,
the church drowned, sunk now inside
a lake spread wide as a dream,
though the lost still found their way
twice in a decade, urged in
by old currents, eyes open,
as if deep in wonder when
divers fell like dark angels
read death in braille, warm hand curled
to close those eyes before brought
back to the light of the world.

APPALACHIAN CHRIST

Tongues of stone break the green silence,
reunion over. I leave those who left me,
enter the church to frame a memory.
More critical now, the cross off-plumb,
the torso too long, the arms clumsy muscled,
bloodless palms open in surrender.
Local color predominates: cross-wood
white pine, the crown green blackberry briar.
Blue Ridge constellations pierce heaven,
James Rash, 1940, printed in the corner.
The arrested face captures my attention,
visage gaunt, unsunned. I look closer.
Glass mirrors grey eyes that mark our clan,
the eyes looking up, seeking a distant father.

October on Middlefork Creek

All night I lay beside water,
my face turned to its flow, so easy
to let my dreams follow its glide
through Watauga County, the mountains
that shadow my ancestors' sleep
in two cemeteries, one row
of creek stones in a pasture.
The dead seem so close this cold dawn
as fawnlight drifts in the trees,
each yellow poplar leaf glows
like a struck match, and fog lifts
off the stream like risen souls.

CATAMOUNT

They will tell you the last one was killed
near Bryson City in 1930, ranging now
only across black and white photographs
in the hollows of the state museum,
so the biologists say and offer
seven decades and no track confirmed
in riversand or snow, no scat,
no deer covered in tree-fall, the neck
crusted black with arterial blood.
But I know one believer
who walked out of Graveyard Fields
where the Pigeon River's West Fork springs,
a big cat padding above on the cliff,
long tail brushing rock as it tensed,
changed its mind and vanishing
left its print on a man given
vision beyond human measure.

AMONG THE BELIEVERS

Even the young back then died old.
My great-aunt's brow at twenty-eight
was labored by a hardscrabble world
no final breath could smooth away.
They laid her out in her wedding dress,
the life that killed in her arms, the head
turned to suckle her cold breast
in eternity. A cousin held
a camera above the open casket,
cast a shadow the camera raised
where flesh and wood and darkness met,
a photograph the husband claimed.
Nailed on the wall above his bed,
smudged and traced for five decades,
a cross of shadow, shadowing death,
across an uncomprehending face.

GOOD FRIDAY, 1995, DRIVING WESTWARD

This day I feel I live among strangers.
The old blood ties beckon so I drive west
to Buncombe County, a weedy graveyard
where my rare last name crumbles on stone.

All were hardshell Baptists, farmers
who believed the soul is another seed
that endures when flesh and blood are shed,
that all things planted rise toward the sun.

I dream them shaking dirt off strange new forms.
Gathered for the last harvest, they hold hands,
take their first dazed steps toward heaven.

Notes

PAGE 3: "On the Border": *Albion's Seed*, David Fischer: "One Scottish army struggled home so laden with loot soldiers drowned in the River Eden."

PAGE 11: "Madison County, 1864": *Bushwackers: The Civil War in North Carolina*, William Trotter: "If you've got to die, die like a damned dog — with your teeth in somebody's throat."

PAGE 12: "Allen's Command": *Bushwackers: The Civil War in North Carolina*, William Trotter: "Woods begged, 'At least give us time to pray!'"

PAGE 13: "On the Watauga": *The Mabinogion*, translation by Jeffrey Gantz: "on the bank of the river he saw a tall tree: from roots to crown one half was aflame and the other green with leaves."

PAGE 14: "Before": *Albion's Seed*, David Fischer: "When the last moment came, the dying person was gently lifted from the bed and lowered to the floor."

PAGE 24: "The Language of Canaan": *Southern Cross*, Christine Leigh Heyrman: "forcing a luxurient bloom of assurance in their barren souls."

PAGE 41: "From *The Mabinogion*": *The Mabinogion* is a book of anonymous and heroic tales that date from the medieval period which the Welsh regard as their equivalent of the *Illiad* and the *Odyssey*.

Biographical Note

Ron Rash's family has lived in the southern Appalachian mountains since the mid-1700's, and it is this region that is the primary focus of his writing. Rash grew up in Boiling Springs, North Carolina, and graduated from Gardner-Webb College and Clemson University. He now lives in Clemson, South Carolina, with his wife and two children. He teaches English at Tri-County Technical College and teaches poetry at the South Carolina Governor's School for the Arts.

In 1987 his fiction won a General Electric Younger Writers Award and in 1994 he was awarded an NEA Poetry Fellowship. He was awarded the Sherwood Anderson Prize in 1996. His poetry and fiction have appeared in a number of journals, including *Yale Review, Georgia Review, Oxford American, New England Review, Southern Review, Shenandoah* and *DoubleTake*. He is the author of two previous books, *The Night The New Jesus Fell to Earth*, a collection of stories, and *Eureka Mill*, a collection of poems.

This book was typeset in Sabon. A descendant of the types of Claude Garamond, Sabon was designed by Jan Tschichold in 1964 and jointly released by Stempel, Linotype, and Monotype foundries. The roman design is based on a Garamond specimen printed by Konrad F. Berner, who was married to the widow of another printer, Jacques Sabon. The italic design is based on types by Robert Granjon, a contemporary of Garamond's.

♾ The paper in this book is recycled and meets the guidelines for permanence and durability of the Committee on Production Guidelines for Book Longevity of the Council on Library Resources.

printed in the United States of America
by Thomson-Shore, Inc.